3-D THR[...]

SOLAR SYSTEM

DUTTON CHILDREN'S BOOKS
NEW YORK

HOME SWEET HOME

i f someone asked where you live, you'd probably give your street address. But you could answer that question in a way that every living thing on Earth or on any of the other eight planets could, too. We all live in the solar system.

AROUND THE SUN

Greek astronomer Aristarchus (ca. 310–230 B.C.) was the first person to claim that the Earth revolves around the Sun. However, Polish astronomer Nicolaus Copernicus (1473–1543), above, usually gets the credit. Few people believed Copernicus's theory in his lifetime. It wasn't until German astronomer Johannes Kepler (1571–1630) showed that planetary motions best fit the Sun-centered nature of the solar system that the idea began to gain acceptance.

THE SOLAR SYSTEM

At the center of our solar system is the Sun, a medium-sized star called a yellow dwarf. Earth and the other planets orbit, or travel, around the Sun. Each planet also spins on its axis, an imaginary line through the center of the planet, like a top. Besides the Sun and planets, the solar system also includes moons, meteoroids, asteroids, and comets.

THE MILKY WAY

Our solar system is part of the Milky Way galaxy.
A galaxy is a cluster of hundreds of billions of
stars, plus dust, different types of gas, and
empty space. From Earth, the Milky Way appears
as a soft glowing band of light encircling the sky.
It got its name in ancient times when people
thought it looked like a stream of milk in the
night sky.

LIGHT-YEARS AWAY

Because the universe is so big, it's not always helpful
to measure distance in space the same way as on
Earth. Instead of miles and kilometers, astronomers
often use light-years. Light is the fastest type of
energy in the universe, so it is able to travel a lot
farther than all other forces. A light-year is the
distance light travels in one Earth year—5.9 trillion
miles (9.5 trillion kilometers)! The Andromeda galaxy
(above), the closest spiral galaxy to ours, is 2.2
million light-years away.

All the stars in the night sky that
we can see from Earth are in the
Milky Way. However, there are
about 50 billion galaxies in the
universe, some much bigger
than the Milky Way. There
are stars in all of them, and
who knows? Maybe one of
those stars is the Sun for
another planet with life
like Earth's.

THE ORIGINAL

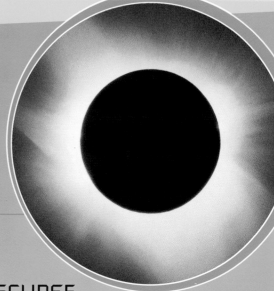

H ot news: Even on the coldest night in the coldest winter in Antarctica, the Sun is giving heat. Life on Earth could not exist without the Sun, even when you don't see it or feel it.

ONE AMONG MANY

Our Sun is a star, a giant sphere of swirling, burning gases (mostly hydrogen and helium). Because it's the closest star to Earth, it gets a lot of attention. However, the Sun is not so special when compared to all the stars in the universe. Every twinkling dot in the sky is another star, some much bigger than our Sun. But our Sun is pretty big in its own right—about 865,000 miles (1,392,000 kilometers) wide. Over one million Earths could fit inside it.

SOLAR ECLIPSE

When the Moon passes between Earth and the Sun, it casts a shadow that passes over a small part of Earth, creating a solar eclipse. In a total solar eclipse you can't see the Sun; you're in the darkest part of the shadow and it will feel like night. If you can still see part of the Sun, you're experiencing a partial solar eclipse. An annular eclipse is when you can see a ring of Sun around the black disk of the moon. Eclipses usually last about three minutes and not longer than seven minutes, forty seconds. Before science explained eclipses, some people thought a monster was devouring the Sun!

On August 11, 1999, people from England to India were plunged into temporary darkness during a highly publicized total solar eclipse that lasted a little over two minutes. They were lucky to see it! Some countries will have to wait about 80 years before another total eclipse comes along. Other areas of the world, including the northeastern United States, saw a partial solar eclipse.

Superstar

GAS, GAS, AND MORE GAS

Three distinct layers of gas cover the Sun. The photosphere is its surface—and is what we can see at any time. The chromosphere is the glowing layer of gas that extends several thousand miles above the photosphere. The corona is the outermost part of the Sun's atmosphere. Its edge is about 10 million miles (16 million kilometers) out from the Sun. Both the chromosphere and the corona are visible to the naked eye only during total solar eclipses.

A DAZZLING DISPLAY

The Sun puts on enormous fireworks shows all the time. Solar flares are short bursts of light from the chromosphere that reach into the corona. Solar prominences (right) are stringy gas clouds that extend from the photosphere into the corona and can last several weeks. Dark blotches on the Sun's surface, called sunspots (above, top right), are places where the gas is cooler. A single sunspot can be larger than the Earth.

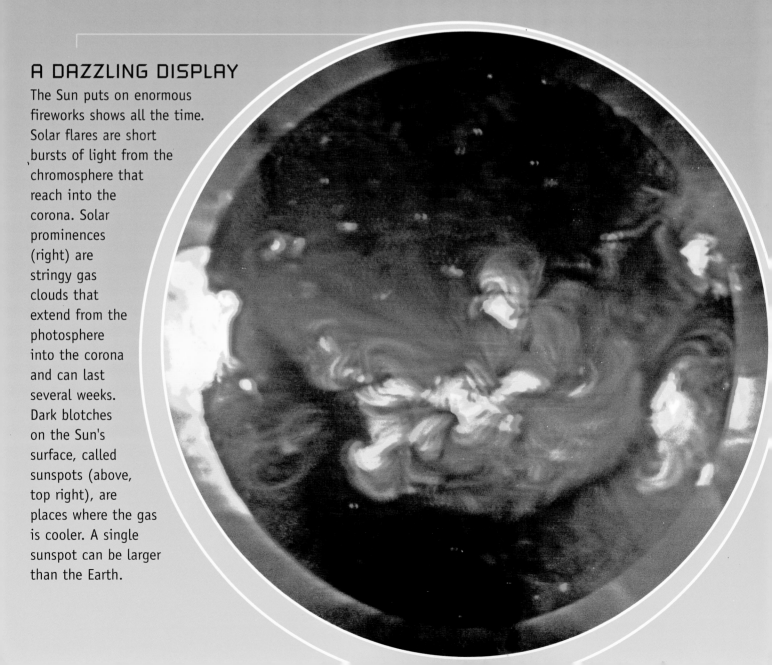

THE HOSPITABLE PLANET

Earth is the third planet from the Sun, which is just the right distance for living organisms to have enough—but not too much— heat and light to live. There are very hot and cold areas on Earth, but on the whole our planet's very livable. Location is everything. Venus, one stop closer to the Sun, is too hot, while Mars, one stop farther from the Sun, is too cold. The temperature on Earth is just right for water to be liquid.

No one knows for sure how the Moon was formed. Some believe a large comet or asteroid slammed into Earth. The debris formed a ring around Earth that coalesced into the Moon.

T he only places in the solar system where humans have walked are Earth and its Moon.

Oceans of water cover over 70 percent of our planet's surface. Earth is the only planet with oceans of liquid water, though some other planets and some moons may have liquid water beneath their icy surfaces. It was in this ocean that life first began on Earth. Now our planet is home to billions and billions of living things found nowhere else in the solar system and, possibly, the universe.

A GIANT STEP

In 1969, as commander of the Apollo 11 mission, Neil Armstrong (born 1930) of Ohio became the first person to set foot on the Moon. Only eleven other men have done the same, during the course of six more Apollo missions. The last one was in 1972. Each mission had a three-man crew, but each time only two got the chance to walk on the Moon. The third stayed in the orbiting ship.

The Moon may have ice mixed in with soil at its poles. Even if there is water on the Moon, it still could not support life because it has no atmosphere. Temperature on the moon ranges from 261°F (117°C) at noon to -279°F (-169°C) just before daybreak.

PHASES OF THE MOON

The Moon never looks the same as it did the day before, because it goes through phases every month, from crescent (sliver) to quarter moon to full moon to new moon (which looks like no moon). Of course the Moon doesn't actually change shape; just our view of it does. The Moon has no light of its own—what we see as moonlight is a reflection of the Sun's light shining on the Moon. As the Moon orbits the Earth, we see more and more (or less and less) of its bright face.

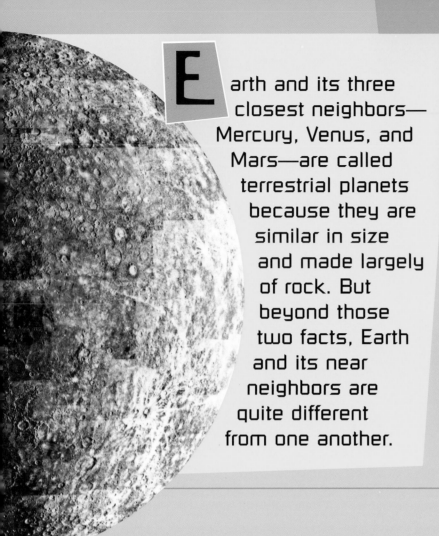

GOOD

E arth and its three closest neighbors—Mercury, Venus, and Mars—are called terrestrial planets because they are similar in size and made largely of rock. But beyond those two facts, Earth and its near neighbors are quite different from one another.

MERCURY

At a distance of 36 million miles (58 million kilometers), Mercury (left) is the closest planet to the Sun. It is the second-smallest planet (Pluto is the smallest) and has no moons. Mercury has the biggest temperature range of all planets, from -297°F (-183°C) at night to 845°F (452°C) during the day! One Mercury day equals 59 Earth days (meaning it takes Mercury 59 Earth days to rotate once on its axis). Mercury's landscape is covered with craters and was photographed and researched by the unmanned space probe *Mariner 10* in 1974 and 1975.

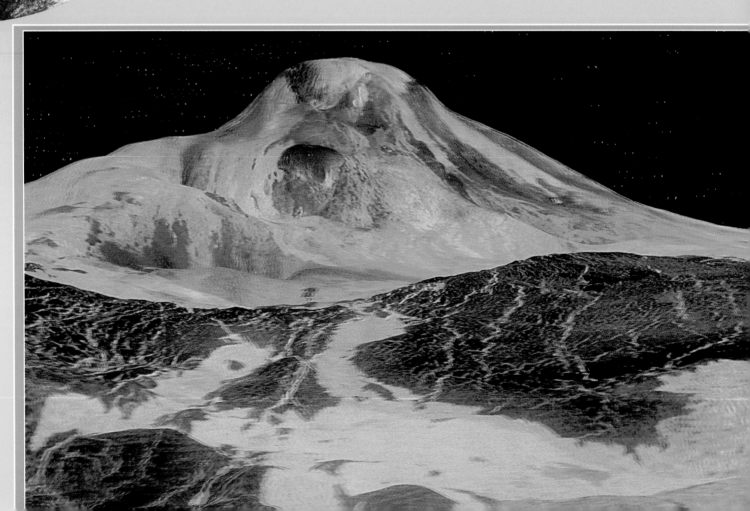

NEiGHBORS

Is there life on Mars? Most likely not. Has there been? Possibly. Small markings that look like fossilized bacteria have been found on a very old rock believed to be from Mars.

MARS

Scientists hope to land humans on Mars, the fourth planet from the Sun, within your lifetime. The Mars day is about half an hour longer than an Earth day, but its year lasts 687 days. Its atmosphere is mostly carbon dioxide, with little oxygen and a high level of radiation. There are also frequent dust storms. Mars has two moons and is about half the size of Earth. Its red color comes from iron in its soil. In other words, Mars is rusty, as well as harsh.

VENUS

Venus is the second planet from the Sun and is the brightest object in the sky after the Sun and Moon. It can often be seen just after dark or at dawn and is also called the "evening star" or "morning star." Venus is the hottest planet in the solar system—with temperatures as high as 895°F (480°C). Not only does it rotate from east to west, which means the Sun rises in the west and sets in the east, its year is shorter than its day! This means it travels around the Sun quicker than it rotates once on its axis. Venus has a string of volcanoes along its equator, including Maat Mons (left). None are known to be active.

VISIT TO MARS

In 1976, two unmanned probes, *Viking 1* and *Viking 2*, landed on Mars to search for signs of life. They found none. *Viking 2* sent back the above image of the planet's red, rock-strewn landscape. Mars is also home to the solar system's tallest mountain, Olympus Mons, an extinct volcano fifteen times taller than Mount Everest.

THE GAS GIANTS

The solar system's powerhouse pair is Jupiter and Saturn. Jupiter is the biggest planet, with Saturn a close second. Like the next two planets from the Sun, Uranus and Neptune, they are made of gases (primarily hydrogen in metallic and liquid form) with cores of rock or rock and ice. All four of these gas giants—not just Saturn—have rings!

MOONS

Eighteen named moons revolve around Jupiter, almost as if it is the center of a solar system of its own. It may have even more moons waiting to be located. In 1610 Italian astronomer Galileo Galilei (1564–1642) discovered four of Jupiter's moons: Callisto, Europa, Ganymede, and Io. Each can be seen from Earth with binoculars. Europa is covered with water ice under which may be an ocean of liquid water—that ocean may contain life. Io (above) is the only other place in the solar system besides Earth known to have active volcanoes.

JUPITER

Jupiter is the fifth planet from the sun. Its day is only about ten hours long. In fact, it spins so fast that it bulges at its equator. The Giant Red Spot, a red swirling circle seen on Jupiter, is a storm over 8,500 miles (14,000 kilometers) wide and 16,000 miles (26,000 kilometers) long—big enough to cover two Earths! Jupiter itself is thirteen hundred times larger than Earth. As if a constant storm isn't stressful enough, fragments of Comet Shoemaker-Levy 9 bombarded the planet in an exciting six-day event in 1994. One collision produced an eruption 100,000 times more powerful than the largest nuclear bomb ever detonated.

SATURN

If you think Jupiter's eighteen moons are a lot, Saturn has twenty, and possibly many more not yet discovered. Like Jupiter, Saturn spins very fast. Lasting ten hours, thirty-nine minutes, its day is a little longer than Jupiter's, but still less than half as long as Earth's. Like Earth, Saturn has auroras in the polar regions (right), which extend about 2,000 miles (3,200 kilometers) above the clouds. Saturn's average density is less than that of water, so it would float if you dropped it into a big enough ocean or pool.

SEEING TRIPLE

Saturn is the sixth planet from the Sun but is almost twice as far away from the Sun as Jupiter. When Galileo first observed Saturn in 1610, he thought he was seeing three planets. Through Galileo's telescope, Saturn's rings looked like two other planets on either side of Saturn. In 1659, Dutch astronomer Christiaan Huygens (1629–1695) confirmed that it was actually one planet with rings. The rings are made of ice, frozen gas, and rock. The rings are not solid—you can see stars through them. Scientists estimate that the rings are at most one mile (1.6 kilometers) thick.

GRILLED *GALILEO*

In 1989, the space shuttle *Atlantis* launched the *Galileo* miniprobe, only the size of a barbecue grill. Six years later, in 1995, it entered Jupiter's atmosphere as planned and sent back measurements and other data. After eight hours, it got so hot that the probe vaporized. Yet thanks to this brave little probe, we now know a lot more about Jupiter.

Distant Relatives

The three outermost planets—Neptune, Uranus, and Pluto—are a mixed bunch. Uranus and Neptune are similar to Jupiter and Saturn, and Pluto has similarities to the terrestrial planets. They're all very far away, and much of what we know about them was learned only recently.

URANUS

Uranus is the third-largest planet in the solar system, the seventh from the Sun, and four times as large as Earth. It has fifteen named moons and eleven rings (right). Uranus is twice as far from the Sun as Saturn, so when German astronomer William Herschel (1738–1822) accidentally discovered it in 1781, it doubled the size of our solar system! In 1978, another startling discovery was made: like Saturn, Uranus has rings, also made of dust, rocks, and ice. However, they are thin and dark and harder to see than Saturn's.

Some people think there is another large, but elusive, planet beyond Pluto whose gravitational pull affects the orbits of Uranus and Neptune. If such a planet exists, it may be too far for our telescopes to see, or it may take close to one thousand years to orbit the Sun and may not come into view anytime soon. Like many other things about our solar system, it remains a mystery.

TWO POLES TO THE SUN

Much else that we know about Uranus was not learned until 1986, when *Voyager 2* passed by. Its atmosphere is made mostly of hydrogen and methane. Since it is so far from the Sun, it is also very cold. The average temperature is just -353°F (-214°C). Perhaps Uranus's oddest feature is that it is sideways! Unlike Earth, its north and south poles face the Sun. When one Uranus pole faces the Sun, the other pole is in complete darkness for half a Uranus year—42 Earth years!

TRITON

The large south polar cap on Neptune's largest moon, Triton, is thought to consist of a slowly evaporating layer of nitrogen ice.

NEPTUNE

Neptune, the eighth planet, is a billion miles from Uranus. It was named after the Roman god of the sea because of its rich blue hue. However, it is not water but methane gas that gives Neptune its color. Neptune is not only cold (average temperature is -364°F, -220°C) but windy, too. Winds whip around the planet at 1,500 mph—the fastest in the solar system. *Voyager 2* discovered six of Neptune's eight named moons and its rings. Although Neptune is usually the eighth planet, sometimes Pluto's orbit crosses inside Neptune's and Neptune is farthest from the Sun. Pluto was closer to the Sun than Neptune from 1979 until 1999.

PLUTO

The last and the least (in size, anyway) planet is Pluto. Because it is so small and its orbit is so irregular, some scientists don't consider Pluto a planet but more like a comet. American astronomer Clyde Tombaugh (1906–1997) discovered Pluto in 1930, although another American astronomer, Percival Lowell (1855–1916), had predicted its existence by 1905. Pluto has not yet been visited by spacecraft. Pluto is named after the Roman god of the underworld, and its only moon, Charon, which was discovered as recently as 1978, is named after the character in Roman mythology that took souls by boat to Hades.

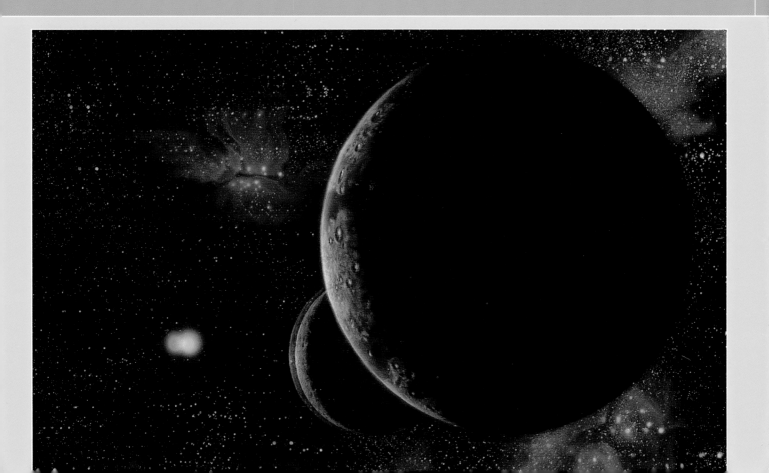

ROCKETING ROCKS

Planets, moons, and stars have many smaller companions in space: asteroids, comets, and meteoroids. They are the rock stars of space, but let's hope they never have a greatest hit.

ASTEROIDS

Asteroids (also called minor planets) are rocky chunks that orbit the Sun. There are an estimated one million of them in our solar system, mostly in the belt between Mars and Jupiter. Scientists once thought that asteroids were remains of a planet that exploded. Now most agree that asteroids are fragments that have been around since the formation of our solar system but that could not form a planet because nearby Jupiter's gravity was so strong. Most asteroids vary in size from 62 miles (100 kilometers) wide to .6 mile (1 kilometer). Ceres, the largest asteroid at 580 miles (933 kilometers) in diameter, was also the first to be discovered.

Many theorize that the dinosaurs became extinct because an asteroid hit Earth. Such a collision could have sent so much dust into the atmosphere that the Sun's light would have been blocked, thereby killing the plants that dinosaurs ate.

TAIL FIRST

A comet's tail always points away from the Sun, so even when traveling away from the Sun, it shoots tail first. In earlier times, people called comets "hairy stars" and often thought they meant bad luck. In 1995, Comet Hale-Bopp was discovered simultaneously by two American men in different states, and was named after both. It became visible to the naked eye in 1996 and appeared at its brightest in early 1997.

COMETS

Our solar system throws snowballs—they're called comets. A comet is a giant dirty lump of frozen methane, ammonia, and water that orbits the sun on an elliptical path along the edge of the solar system. Comets have long, luminous tails of gas. Comets originate from a spooky-sounding area called the Oort cloud. In 1950, Dutch astronomer Jan Oort (1900–1992) theorized that a region exists beyond Pluto that is a "storage area" for inactive comets.

Halley's comet, which rockets past Earth every 76 years, is probably the most famous comet. Its discoverer, British astronomer Edmund Halley (1656–1742), was the first to recognize that comets follow the same orbits around the Sun again and again. We can next expect Halley's comet in 2061. Mark your calendar!

METEOROIDS

Smaller than asteroids but at least as large as a speck of dust, meteoroids are old stony or metallic particles that travel through space after breaking off from a celestial body such as an asteroid, comet, or planet. Once they enter Earth's atmosphere, they are called meteors. If they hit Earth, they are called meteorites. Many meteors burn up entirely in Earth's atmosphere, but those that make it to the surface are usually smaller than a fist. On occasion they are bigger, and some have caused damage, but only a few of the approximately one million meteorites that hit each year are even seen. It's much safer—and more breathtaking—to see meteorites as meteors. Various meteor showers are visible yearly. The Leonids, for example, put on a show every November.

Discovery Communications, Inc.
John S. Hendricks, *Founder, Chairman, and Chief Executive Officer*
Judith A. McHale, *President and Chief Operating Officer*
Judy L. Harris, *Senior Vice President and General Manager, Consumer Products*
Marjorie Kaplan, *Senior Vice President, Children's Programming and Products*

Discovery Publishing
Natalie Chapman, *Vice President, Publishing*
Rita Thievon Mullin, *Editorial Director*
Tracy Fortini, *Product Development, Discovery Channel Retail*
Heather Quinlan, *Editorial Coordinator*

Discovery Kids™, which includes Saturday and Sunday morning programming on
Discovery Channel®, Discoverykids.com, and the digital showcase network, is dedicated
to encouraging and empowering kids to explore the world around them.

Published in the United States 2001 by Dutton Children's Books,
a division of Penguin Putnam Books for Young Readers
345 Hudson Street, New York, New York 10014
www.penguinputnam.com

Author: Marc T. Nobleman
Editor: Sarah Ketchersid
Consulting Editor: Dr. James Zimbelman, Smithsonian Institution
Designers: Dan Hosek and Susi Martin

Picture Credits:
Julian Baum: front cover.
Bruce Coleman/Michael J Howell: page 2, bottom left.
Galaxy Picture Library: page 3, top right; page 4, bottom left; page 15, top.
Genesis Space Photo Library: page 6, top left; page 8, bottom; page 9, bottom right;
page 10, bottom left.
Robert Harding Picture Library: page 4, top center; page 7, top right; page 13, bottom.
NASA: page 6, bottom right; page 8, top left; page 10, top center; page 12, top center;
page 13, top center; back cover; title page.
Science Photo Library: page 2, top right; A Behrendi/Eurelios, page 15, bottom;
Luke Dodd, page 3, bottom left; Jisas Lockheed, page 5, bottom right; NASA, page 5,
top right; page 11; page 13, top right; Pekka Parviainen, page 16; John Sandford,
page 7, bottom; Joe Tucciarone, page 14, bottom.

3-D images produced by Pinsharp

Printed in China
First Edition
ISBN: 0-525-46469-7